I0461849

2019
Monthly Planner

Belong To :

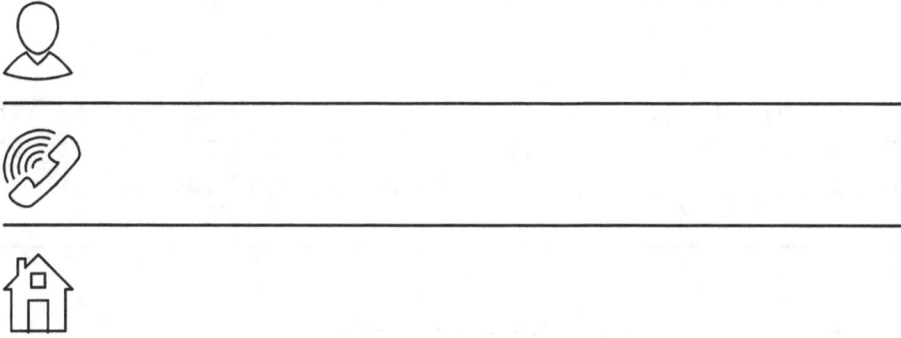

_____

_____

_____

Copyright 2018 - 2019

All rights reserved. No part of this book may be reproduced or transmitted in any form or by any means, electronic or mechanical, including photocopying, recording or by any information storage and retrieval system, without the written permission of the Publisher, except where permitted by law.

CALENDAR 2019

January

Su	Mo	Tu	We	Th	Fr	Sa
		1	2	3	4	5
6	7	8	9	10	11	12
13	14	15	16	17	18	19
20	**21**	22	23	24	25	26
27	28	29	30	31		

February

Su	Mo	Tu	We	Th	Fr	Sa
					1	2
3	4	5	6	7	8	9
10	11	12	13	**14**	15	16
17	**18**	19	20	21	22	23
24	25	26	27	28		

March

Su	Mo	Tu	We	Th	Fr	Sa
					1	2
3	4	5	6	7	8	9
10	11	12	13	14	15	16
17	18	19	20	21	22	23
24	25	26	27	28	29	30
31						

April

Su	Mo	Tu	We	Th	Fr	Sa
	1	2	3	4	5	6
7	8	9	10	11	12	13
14	15	16	17	18	**19**	20
21	22	23	24	25	26	27
28	29	30				

May

Su	Mo	Tu	We	Th	Fr	Sa
		1	2	3	4	
5	6	7	8	9	10	11
12	13	14	15	16	17	18
19	20	21	22	23	24	25
26	**27**	28	29	30	31	

June

Su	Mo	Tu	We	Th	Fr	Sa
						1
2	3	4	5	6	7	8
9	10	11	12	13	14	15
16	17	18	19	20	21	22
23	24	25	26	27	28	29
30						

July

Su	Mo	Tu	We	Th	Fr	Sa
	1	2	3	**4**	5	6
7	8	9	10	11	12	13
14	15	16	17	18	19	20
21	22	23	24	25	26	27
28	29	30	31			

August

Su	Mo	Tu	We	Th	Fr	Sa
				1	2	3
4	5	6	7	8	9	10
11	12	13	14	15	16	17
18	19	20	21	22	23	24
25	26	27	28	29	30	31

September

Su	Mo	Tu	We	Th	Fr	Sa
1	**2**	3	4	5	6	7
8	9	10	11	12	13	14
15	16	17	18	19	20	21
22	23	24	25	26	27	28
29	30					

October

Su	Mo	Tu	We	Th	Fr	Sa
		1	2	3	4	5
6	7	8	9	10	11	12
13	**14**	15	16	17	18	19
20	21	22	23	24	25	26
27	28	29	30	**31**		

November

Su	Mo	Tu	We	Th	Fr	Sa
					1	2
3	4	5	6	7	8	9
10	**11**	12	13	14	15	16
17	18	19	20	21	22	23
24	25	26	27	**28**	29	30

December

Su	Mo	Tu	We	Th	Fr	Sa
1	2	3	4	5	6	7
8	9	10	11	12	13	14
15	16	17	18	19	20	21
22	23	24	**25**	26	27	28
29	30	31				

USA Holidays and Observances

1-Jan	New Year's Day	21-Jan	M L King Day	14-Feb	Valentine's Day
18-Feb	Presidents' Day	19-Apr	Good Friday	21-Apr	Easter Sunday
12-May	Mother's Day	27-May	Memorial Day	16-Jun	Father's Day
4-Jul	Independence Day	2-Sep	Labor Day	14-Oct	Columbus Day
31-Oct	Halloween	11-Nov	Veterans Day	28-Nov	Thanksgiving Day
25-Dec	Christmas				

CALENDAR 2020

January

Su	Mo	Tu	We	Th	Fr	Sa
			1	2	3	4
5	6	7	8	9	10	11
12	13	14	15	16	17	18
19	**20**	21	22	23	24	25
26	27	28	29	30	31	

February

Su	Mo	Tu	We	Th	Fr	Sa
						1
2	3	4	5	6	7	8
9	10	11	12	13	**14**	15
16	**17**	18	19	20	21	22
23	24	25	26	27	28	29

March

Su	Mo	Tu	We	Th	Fr	Sa
1	2	3	4	5	6	7
8	9	10	11	12	13	14
15	16	17	18	19	20	21
22	23	24	25	26	27	28
29	30	31				

April

Su	Mo	Tu	We	Th	Fr	Sa
			1	2	3	4
5	6	7	8	9	**10**	11
12	13	14	15	16	17	18
19	20	21	22	23	24	25
26	27	28	29	30		

May

Su	Mo	Tu	We	Th	Fr	Sa
					1	2
3	4	5	6	7	8	9
10	11	12	13	14	15	16
17	18	19	20	21	22	23
24	**25**	26	27	28	29	30
31						

June

Su	Mo	Tu	We	Th	Fr	Sa
	1	2	3	4	5	6
7	8	9	10	11	12	13
14	15	16	17	18	19	20
21	22	23	24	25	26	27
28	29	30				

July

Su	Mo	Tu	We	Th	Fr	Sa
			1	2	**3**	4
5	6	7	8	9	10	11
12	13	14	15	16	17	18
19	20	21	22	23	24	25
26	27	28	29	30	31	

August

Su	Mo	Tu	We	Th	Fr	Sa
						1
2	3	4	5	6	7	8
9	10	11	12	13	14	15
16	17	18	19	20	21	22
23	24	25	26	27	28	29
30	31					

September

Su	Mo	Tu	We	Th	Fr	Sa
		1	2	3	4	5
6	**7**	8	9	10	11	12
13	14	15	16	17	18	19
20	21	22	23	24	25	26
27	28	29	30			

October

Su	Mo	Tu	We	Th	Fr	Sa
				1	2	3
4	5	6	7	8	9	10
11	**12**	13	14	15	16	17
18	19	20	21	22	23	24
25	26	27	28	29	30	**31**

November

Su	Mo	Tu	We	Th	Fr	Sa
1	2	3	4	5	6	7
8	9	10	**11**	12	13	14
15	16	17	18	19	20	21
22	23	24	25	**26**	27	28
29	30					

December

Su	Mo	Tu	We	Th	Fr	Sa
		1	2	3	4	5
6	7	8	9	10	11	12
13	14	15	16	17	18	19
20	21	22	23	24	**25**	26
27	28	29	30	31		

USA Holidays and Observances

1-Jan	New Year's Day	20-Jan	M L King Day	14-Feb	Valentine's Day
17-Feb	Presidents' Day	10-Apr	Good Friday	12-Apr	Easter Sunday
10-May	Mother's Day	25-May	Memorial Day	21-Jun	Father's Day
3-Jul	Independence Day Holiday	4-Jul	Independence Day	7-Sep	Labor Day
12-Oct	Columbus Day	31-Oct	Halloween	11-Nov	Veterans Day
26-Nov	Thanksgiving Day	25-Dec	Christmas		

2019 Calendar

January	February	March	April	May	June
1 Tu New Year's Day	1 Fr	1 Fr	1 Mo	1 We	1 Sa
2 We	2 Sa	2 Sa	2 Tu	2 Th	2 Su
3 Th	3 Su	3 Su	3 We	3 Fr	3 Mo
4 Fr	4 Mo	4 Mo	4 Th	4 Sa	4 Tu
5 Sa	5 Tu	5 Tu	5 Fr	5 Su	5 We
6 Su	6 We	6 We	6 Sa	6 Mo	6 Th
7 Mo	7 Th	7 Th	7 Su	7 Tu	7 Fr
8 Tu	8 Fr	8 Fr	8 Mo	8 We	8 Sa
9 We	9 Sa	9 Sa	9 Tu	9 Th	9 Su
10 Th	10 Su	10 Su	10 We	10 Fr	10 Mo
11 Fr	11 Mo	11 Mo	11 Th	11 Sa	11 Tu
12 Sa	12 Tu	12 Tu	12 Fr	12 Su	12 We
13 Su	13 We	13 We	13 Sa	13 Mo	13 Th
14 Mo	14 Th	14 Th	14 Su	14 Tu	14 Fr
15 Tu	15 Fr	15 Fr	15 Mo	15 We	15 Sa
16 We	16 Sa	16 Sa	16 Tu	16 Th	16 Su
17 Th	17 Su	17 Su	17 We	17 Fr	17 Mo
18 Fr	18 Mo Presidents' Day	18 Mo	18 Th	18 Sa	18 Tu
19 Sa	19 Tu	19 Tu	19 Fr	19 Su	19 We
20 Su	20 We	20 We	20 Sa	20 Mo	20 Th
21 Mo Martin L. King Day	21 Th	21 Th	21 Su	21 Tu	21 Fr
22 Tu	22 Fr	22 Fr	22 Mo	22 We	22 Sa
23 We	23 Sa	23 Sa	23 Tu	23 Th	23 Su
24 Th	24 Su	24 Su	24 We	24 Fr	24 Mo
25 Fr	25 Mo	25 Mo	25 Th	25 Sa	25 Tu
26 Sa	26 Tu	26 Tu	26 Fr	26 Su	26 We
27 Su	27 We	27 We	27 Sa	27 Mo Memorial Day	27 Th
28 Mo	28 Th	28 Th	28 Su	28 Tu	28 Fr
29 Tu		29 Fr	29 Mo	29 We	29 Sa
30 We		30 Sa	30 Tu	30 Th	30 Su
31 Th		31 Su		31 Fr	

2019 Calendar

July	August	September	October	November	December
1 Mo	1 Th	1 Su	1 Tu	1 Fr	1 Su
2 Tu	2 Fr	2 Mo Labor Day	2 We	2 Sa	2 Mo
3 We	3 Sa	3 Tu	3 Th	3 Su	3 Tu
4 Th Independence Day	4 Su	4 We	4 Fr	4 Mo	4 We
5 Fr	5 Mo	5 Th	5 Sa	5 Tu	5 Th
6 Sa	6 Tu	6 Fr	6 Su	6 We	6 Fr
7 Su	7 We	7 Sa	7 Mo	7 Th	7 Sa
8 Mo	8 Th	8 Su	8 Tu	8 Fr	8 Su
9 Tu	9 Fr	9 Mo	9 We	9 Sa	9 Mo
10 We	10 Sa	10 Tu	10 Th	10 Su	10 Tu
11 Th	11 Su	11 We	11 Fr	11 Mo Veterans Day	11 We
12 Fr	12 Mo	12 Th	12 Sa	12 Tu	12 Th
13 Sa	13 Tu	13 Fr	13 Su	13 We	13 Fr
14 Su	14 We	14 Sa	14 Mo Columbus Day	14 Th	14 Sa
15 Mo	15 Th	15 Su	15 Tu	15 Fr	15 Su
16 Tu	16 Fr	16 Mo	16 We	16 Sa	16 Mo
17 We	17 Sa	17 Tu	17 Th	17 Su	17 Tu
18 Th	18 Su	18 We	18 Fr	18 Mo	18 We
19 Fr	19 Mo	19 Th	19 Sa	19 Tu	19 Th
20 Sa	20 Tu	20 Fr	20 Su	20 We	20 Fr
21 Su	21 We	21 Sa	21 Mo	21 Th	21 Sa
22 Mo	22 Th	22 Su	22 Tu	22 Fr	22 Su
23 Tu	23 Fr	23 Mo	23 We	23 Sa	23 Mo
24 We	24 Sa	24 Tu	24 Th	24 Su	24 Tu
25 Th	25 Su	25 We	25 Fr	25 Mo	25 We Christmas Day
26 Fr	26 Mo	26 Th	26 Sa	26 Tu	26 Th
27 Sa	27 Tu	27 Fr	27 Su	27 We	27 Fr
28 Su	28 We	28 Sa	28 Mo	28 Th Thanksgiving Day	28 Sa
29 Mo	29 Th	29 Su	29 Tu	29 Fr	29 Su
30 Tu	30 Fr	30 Mo	30 We	30 Sa	30 Mo
31 We	31 Sa		31 Th		31 Tu

2020 Calendar

January	February	March	April	May	June
1 We New Year's Day	1 Sa	1 Su	1 We	1 Fr	1 Mo
2 Th	2 Su	2 Mo	2 Th	2 Sa	2 Tu
3 Fr	3 Mo	3 Tu	3 Fr	3 Su	3 We
4 Sa	4 Tu	4 We	4 Sa	4 Mo	4 Th
5 Su	5 We	5 Th	5 Su	5 Tu	5 Fr
6 Mo	6 Th	6 Fr	6 Mo	6 We	6 Sa
7 Tu	7 Fr	7 Sa	7 Tu	7 Th	7 Su
8 We	8 Sa	8 Su	8 We	8 Fr	8 Mo
9 Th	9 Su	9 Mo	9 Th	9 Sa	9 Tu
10 Fr	10 Mo	10 Tu	10 Fr	10 Su	10 We
11 Sa	11 Tu	11 We	11 Sa	11 Mo	11 Th
12 Su	12 We	12 Th	12 Su	12 Tu	12 Fr
13 Mo	13 Th	13 Fr	13 Mo	13 We	13 Sa
14 Tu	14 Fr	14 Sa	14 Tu	14 Th	14 Su
15 We	15 Sa	15 Su	15 We	15 Fr	15 Mo
16 Th	16 Su	16 Mo	16 Th	16 Sa	16 Tu
17 Fr	17 Mo Presidents' Day	17 Tu	17 Fr	17 Su	17 We
18 Sa	18 Tu	18 We	18 Sa	18 Mo	18 Th
19 Su	19 We	19 Th	19 Su	19 Tu	19 Fr
20 Mo Martin L. King Day	20 Th	20 Fr	20 Mo	20 We	20 Sa
21 Tu	21 Fr	21 Sa	21 Tu	21 Th	21 Su
22 We	22 Sa	22 Su	22 We	22 Fr	22 Mo
23 Th	23 Su	23 Mo	23 Th	23 Sa	23 Tu
24 Fr	24 Mo	24 Tu	24 Fr	24 Su	24 We
25 Sa	25 Tu	25 We	25 Sa	25 Mo Memorial Day	25 Th
26 Su	26 We	26 Th	26 Su	26 Tu	26 Fr
27 Mo	27 Th	27 Fr	27 Mo	27 We	27 Sa
28 Tu	28 Fr	28 Sa	28 Tu	28 Th	28 Su
29 We	29 Sa	29 Su	29 We	29 Fr	29 Mo
30 Th		30 Mo	30 Th	30 Sa	30 Tu
31 Fr		31 Tu		31 Su	

2020 Calendar

July	August	September	October	November	December
1 We	1 Sa	1 Tu	1 Th	1 Su	1 Tu
2 Th	2 Su	2 We	2 Fr	2 Mo	2 We
3 Fr Independence Day (observed)	3 Mo	3 Th	3 Sa	3 Tu	3 Th
4 Sa Independence Day	4 Tu	4 Fr	4 Su	4 We	4 Fr
5 Su	5 We	5 Sa	5 Mo	5 Th	5 Sa
6 Mo	6 Th	6 Su	6 Tu	6 Fr	6 Su
7 Tu	7 Fr	7 Mo Labor Day	7 We	7 Sa	7 Mo
8 We	8 Sa	8 Tu	8 Th	8 Su	8 Tu
9 Th	9 Su	9 We	9 Fr	9 Mo	9 We
10 Fr	10 Mo	10 Th	10 Sa	10 Tu	10 Th
11 Sa	11 Tu	11 Fr	11 Su	11 We Veterans Day	11 Fr
12 Su	12 We	12 Sa	12 Mo Columbus Day	12 Th	12 Sa
13 Mo	13 Th	13 Su	13 Tu	13 Fr	13 Su
14 Tu	14 Fr	14 Mo	14 We	14 Sa	14 Mo
15 We	15 Sa	15 Tu	15 Th	15 Su	15 Tu
16 Th	16 Su	16 We	16 Fr	16 Mo	16 We
17 Fr	17 Mo	17 Th	17 Sa	17 Tu	17 Th
18 Sa	18 Tu	18 Fr	18 Su	18 We	18 Fr
19 Su	19 We	19 Sa	19 Mo	19 Th	19 Sa
20 Mo	20 Th	20 Su	20 Tu	20 Fr	20 Su
21 Tu	21 Fr	21 Mo	21 We	21 Sa	21 Mo
22 We	22 Sa	22 Tu	22 Th	22 Su	22 Tu
23 Th	23 Su	23 We	23 Fr	23 Mo	23 We
24 Fr	24 Mo	24 Th	24 Sa	24 Tu	24 Th
25 Sa	25 Tu	25 Fr	25 Su	25 We	25 Fr Christmas Day
26 Su	26 We	26 Sa	26 Mo	26 Th Thanksgiving Day	26 Sa
27 Mo	27 Th	27 Su	27 Tu	27 Fr	27 Su
28 Tu	28 Fr	28 Mo	28 We	28 Sa	28 Mo
29 We	29 Sa	29 Tu	29 Th	29 Su	29 Tu
30 Th	30 Su	30 We	30 Fr	30 Mo	30 We
31 Fr	31 Mo		31 Sa		31 Th

PLAN		1	2	3	4	5	6	7	8	9	10	11	12	13	14

JAN
2019

SUN	MON	TUE
		1 New Year's Day
6	7	8
13	14	15
20	21 M L King Day	22
27	28	29

_____
_____
_____
_____
_____
_____
_____
_____
_____
_____
_____
_____
_____
_____

15	16	17	18	19	20	21	22	23	24	25	26	27	28	29	30	31

WED	THU	FRI	SAT
2	3	4	5
9	10	11	12
16	17	18	19
23	24	25	26
30	31		

PLAN	1	2	3	4	5	6	7	8	9	10	11	12	13	14

FEB
2019

SUN	MON	TUE
3	4	5
10	11	12
17	18	19
	Presidents' Day	
24	25	26

_____
_____
_____
_____
_____
_____
_____
_____
_____
_____
_____

15	16	17	18	19	20	21	22	23	24	25	26	27	28	29	30	31

WED	THU	FRI	SAT
		1	2
6	7	8	9
13	14	15	16
	Valentine's Day		
20	21	22	23
27	28		

MAR
2019

SUN	MON	TUE
3	4	5
10	11	12
17	18	19
31 / 24	25	26

15	16	17	18	19	20	21	22	23	24	25	26	27	28	29	30	31

WED	THU	FRI	SAT
		1	2
6	7	8	9
13	14	15	16
20	21	22	23
27	28	29	30

APR
2019

SUN	MON	TUE
	1	2
7	8	9
14	15	16
21	22	23
28 Easter Sunday	29	30

15	16	17	18	19	20	21	22	23	24	25	26	27	28	29	30	31

WED	THU	FRI	SAT
3	4	5	6
10	11	12	13
17	18	19 Good Friday	20
24	25	26	27

PLAN	1	2	3	4	5	6	7	8	9	10	11	12	13	14

MAY
2019

SUN	MON	TUE
5	6	7
12	13	14
Mother's Day		
19	20	21
26	27	28
	Memorial Day	

_____
_____
_____
_____
_____
_____
_____
_____
_____
_____
_____
_____
_____

15	16	17	18	19	20	21	22	23	24	25	26	27	28	29	30	31

WED	THU	FRI	SAT
1	2	3	4
8	9	10	11
15	16	17	18
22	23	24	25
29	30	31	

JUN
2019

SUN	MON	TUE
2	3	4
9	10	11
16	17	18
Father's Day 30 / 23	24	25

15	16	17	18	19	20	21	22	23	24	25	26	27	28	29	30	31

WED	THU	FRI	SAT
			1
5	6	7	8
12	13	14	15
19	20	21	22
26	27	28	29

JULY
2019

SUN	MON	TUE
	1	2
7	8	9
14	15	16
21	22	23
28	29	30

15	16	17	18	19	20	21	22	23	24	25	26	27	28	29	30	31

WED	THU	FRI	SAT
3	4	5	6
	Independence Day		
10	11	12	13
17	18	19	20
24	25	26	27
31			

PLAN		1	2	3	4	5	6	7	8	9	10	11	12	13	14

AUG
2019

SUN	MON	TUE
4	5	6
11	12	13
18	19	20
25	26	27

_____

_____

_____

_____

_____

_____

_____

_____

_____

_____

_____

_____

15	16	17	18	19	20	21	22	23	24	25	26	27	28	29	30	31

WED	THU	FRI	SAT
	1	2	3
7	8	9	10
14	15	16	17
21	22	23	24
28	29	30	31

PLAN		1	2	3	4	5	6	7	8	9	10	11	12	13	14

SEP
2019

SUN	MON	TUE
1	2 Labor Day	3
8	9	10
15	16	17
22	23	24
29	30	

_____
_____
_____
_____
_____
_____
_____
_____
_____
_____
_____
_____
_____

15	16	17	18	19	20	21	22	23	24	25	26	27	28	29	30	31

WED	THU	FRI	SAT
4	5	6	7
11	12	13	14
18	19	20	21
25	26	27	28

PLAN	1	2	3	4	5	6	7	8	9	10	11	12	13	14

OCT
2019

SUN	MON	TUE
		1
6	7	8
13	14 Columbus Day	15
20	21	22
27	28	29

_____
_____
_____
_____
_____
_____
_____
_____
_____
_____
_____
_____
_____

15	16	17	18	19	20	21	22	23	24	25	26	27	28	29	30	31

WED	THU	FRI	SAT
2	3	4	5
9	10	11	12
16	17	18	19
23	24	25	26
30	31 Halloween		

PLAN	1	2	3	4	5	6	7	8	9	10	11	12	13	14

NOV
2019

SUN	MON	TUE
3	4	5
10	11	12
	Veterans Day	
17	18	19
24	25	26

	15	16	17	18	19	20	21	22	23	24	25	26	27	28	29	30	31

WED	THU	FRI	SAT
		1	2
6	7	8	9
13	14	15	16
20	21	22	23
27	28 Thanksgiving Day	29	30

PLAN	1	2	3	4	5	6	7	8	9	10	11	12	13	14

DEC
2019

SUN	MON	TUE
1	2	3
8	9	10
15	16	17
22	23	24
29	30	31

15	16	17	18	19	20	21	22	23	24	25	26	27	28	29	30	31

WED	THU	FRI	SAT
4	5	6	7
11	12	13	14
18	19	20	21
25 Christmas Day	26	27	28

www.ingramcontent.com/pod-product-compliance
Lightning Source LLC
Chambersburg PA
CBHW081303180526
45170CB00007B/2551